John Buscema Artist & Inker

by Sue Hamilton

Visit us at
www.abdopublishing.com

Published by ABDO Publishing Company, 4940 Viking Drive, Suite 622, Edina, Minnesota 55435.
Copyright ©2007 by Abdo Consulting Group, Inc. International copyrights reserved in all countries.
No part of this book may be reproduced in any form without written permission from the publisher.
ABDO & Daughters™ is a trademark and logo of ABDO Publishing Company.

Printed in the United States.

Editor: John Hamilton
Graphic Design: Sue Hamilton
Cover Design: Neil Klinepier
Cover Illustration: John Buscema, courtesy the Buscema family.
Interior Photos and Illustrations: pp 1–32 All Marvel comic book character and cover images used
with permission from Marvel Entertainment, Inc.
pp 1, 5-6, 10-11, 13-15, 18, 20, 23, 25-29, 31, photos of John Buscema, his family, and artwork,
courtesy the Buscema family.
p 7 Brooklyn Museum, Getty Images; p 9 Empire State Building, Getty Images.
p 19 Jack Kirby, courtesy the Kirby family.

Library of Congress Cataloging-in-Publication Data

Hamilton, Sue L., 1959-
  John Buscema / Sue Hamilton.
    p. cm. -- (Comic book creators)
  Includes bibliographical references and index.
  ISBN-13: 978-1-59928-297-8
  ISBN-10: 1-59928-297-6
  1. Buscema, John--Juvenile literature. 2. Cartoonists--United States--Biography--Juvenile literature.
I. Title. II. Series: Hamilton, Sue L., 1959- Comic book creators.

  PN6727.B88Z63 2006
  741.5'092--dc22
  [B]
                              2006015407

Contents

John Buscema was a Marvel Comics artist who specialized in drawing the human form. He studied history's master painters, and from that style created such formidable heroes as Conan the Barbarian, The Silver Surfer, and The Mighty Thor. A bear of a man, "Big" John Buscema created big comic book successes. Millions of fans knew that when they bought his comic books, they'd find amazing characters and stories full of action and adventure.

John Natale (Italian for "Christmas") Buscema was born December 11, 1927, to John and Rosaria "Sadie" Buscema in Brooklyn, New York. John's father owned a barbershop, and his mom was a homemaker.

Right: Conan the Barbarian #149, featuring cover art by John Buscema.

Above: "Big" John Buscema teaches a drawing class at a summer art school in Oneonta, New York, 1993.

One of five kids, John began drawing as a child. Although he enjoyed reading and playing sports, he really loved to draw. By the time John was 10 years old, he was studying newspaper comic strips. He loved Hal Foster's *Prince Valiant in the Days of King Arthur*, Alex Raymond's *Flash Gordon,* and Burne Hogarth's *Tarzan.*

In 1939, when John was 11 years old, he read his first *Superman* comic book. This was the comic that brought the industry to life. Within a few years, comics were big business. But John didn't want to be a comic book artist. He quit reading comic books in his early teens. John wanted to be a painter.

Art Schools & Museums

As John became more interested in art, he attended the High School of Music and Art, which was founded in 1936 by New York's Mayor Fiorello H. LaGuardia. Buscema didn't stop with his high school classes. In the mid-1940s, he spent more than a year and a half attending classes at the Pratt Institute, a New York learning center whose students were taught trades through the "skillful use of their hands." John studied life drawing and design.

His education also included trips to New York's museums. From the Metropolitan Museum of Art to the Brooklyn Museum, Buscema studied the paintings of such masters as Michelangelo and Leonardo da Vinci. John also enjoyed the works of some of America's modern painters, including Norman Rockwell and Al Dorne, both of whom worked for the popular *Saturday Evening Post* magazine.

But everything changed in 1948 when John read a help wanted ad in the *New York Times* newspaper.

Above: John Buscema (left) with a friend in 1950.

Above: The Brooklyn Museum, where John Buscema spent many hours studying artistic works.

Timely Comics

In 1948, 21-year-old John was trying to get work, and it wasn't easy. John's father had warned him that his choice of careers would be difficult, but Buscema's mother continued to encourage her son. Then one day, John read a help wanted ad in the *New York Times* newspaper.

Taking along samples of his work, John went to the Timely Comics offices in New York City. (The company was first called Timely Comics, and then Atlas Comics, before publisher Martin Goodman settled on the name Marvel Comics.) Buscema met with Stan Lee, the editor, and before John left, he had his first full time job in comics. Stan would also be the one to give John the nickname of "Big" John Buscema.

John became part of the staff, working on the 14th floor of the Empire State Building. With a nice salary of $75 per week, he began the task of creating comic books.

Crime comic books were very popular. John began working on *All-True Crime* and *Justice*. These included stories of criminals, their beautiful molls (girlfriends), police, and the "true cases proving crime can't win!" John drew guys, girls, and guns. He quickly realized that he needed to be fast to get the job done on deadline. He did just that, getting quicker and better with every issue.

Westerns were also popular, and John was called on to create cowboy tales of danger and dust. He worked on such titles as *Tex Morgan* and *Western Outlaws and Sheriffs*.

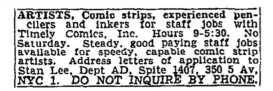

ARTISTS, Comic strips, experienced pencillers and inkers for staff jobs with Timely Comics, Inc. Hours 9-5:30. No Saturday. Steady, good paying staff jobs available for speedy, capable comic strip artists. Address letters of application to Stan Lee, Dept AD, Spite 1407, 350 5 Av, NYC 1. DO NOT INQUIRE BY PHONE.

Above: A Timely Comics ad that ran in the *New York Times* in the late 1940s.

Left: The Empire State Building in New York City, 1946. John Buscema worked for Timely Comics on the 14th floor of this famous office building in 1948.

For a year and a half, John worked and learned from some of Timely's talented staff artists. John was happy working at Timely. But one day, publisher Martin Goodman discovered a closet full of unused work, which had been produced but never printed. He thought this was wasteful, and decided to make a change. The artists would be paid job-to-job, on a "freelance," per-page basis. Technically, they would not be employed by Timely.

Suddenly, Buscema no longer had a regular job. However, instead of this being a bad thing, it opened up many new opportunities.

Working From A to Z

Buscema began working from home. He continued penciling, drawing rough pencil images, for Timely/Atlas (the company's name was changing), but he also began taking jobs from other publishers as well.

Orbit, Ziff-Davis, Dell Comics, and Our Publishing wanted John's work. He was so busy that he hired other people to help him get the work done. He penciled the pages, then "inkers" traced his rough pencil images with black India ink.

In addition to drawing crime and Westerns, he also worked on mysteries and suspense comics, including *Strange Tales*, *Tales to Astonish*, and *Mystic*. John drew everything from aliens to zombies, producing such stories as "The Corpse That Wasn't" and "Don't Lose Your Head." He didn't stop there.

John also worked on comics for young ladies.

When romance comics were first published in the early 1950s, John took his turn at drawing the beautiful women and men in *My Own Romance, My Romantic Adventures*, and *Love Journal*. With titles such as "Ladies' Man" and "Make Way For Love, " he created beautiful graphic stories. It was at this time that he was about to have his own romance.

Right: John and his future wife, Dolores Celecia, after she graduated from nursing school in 1952.

Above: John Buscema in the Army, with his parents, John and Sadie, 1951.

In 1950, John attended a dance in Brooklyn, New York. He met Dolores Celecia, a young woman in her second year of nursing school. They began dating, but the Korean War interrupted their romance.

John was drafted into the U.S. Army. As a skilled artist, he produced artwork for the Army's Ordnance Corps, which supported fighting servicemen by supplying arms and ammunition. However, John's time in the service was limited. After five months, he received a medical discharge due to stomach ulcers.

John returned to civilian life, picked up his comic book work, and continued dating Dolores. The two were married on November 28, 1953.

These were good months, as the artist and the nurse began their lives together. Unfortunately, this was right before the comic book industry became very unpopular.

Comics Code Authority

In early 1954, the comic book industry was accused of using too much violence and gore. Psychologist Fredric Wertham worked with many delinquent children and discovered that all of the kids had read comic books. It didn't seem to matter to him that nearly every kid in America read comics. Wertham published *Seduction of the Innocent*, a book that claimed comics harmed children.

Wertham pointed the finger at horror and crime comics, but many people thought *all* comics were harmful. On April 21, 1954, a subcommittee of the Senate Judiciary Committee opened hearings to determine if comic books caused juvenile delinquency. Several medical professionals stepped forward to argue this wasn't true. But the damage to the comic book business had been done. Parents believed that comics were bad. This resulted in a huge decrease in sales.

Suddenly, nearly everyone in comics, including John Buscema, found it difficult to keep steady work. Many comic book companies went out of business. Only the best-selling comics continued to be produced and sold.

Later in 1954, the Comics Magazine Association of America was formed, made up of the remaining comic book publishers. Very specific rules were created, and every comic book had to go through the Comics Code Authority (CCA) for approval. Comic books that followed the rules could display the seal of approval on the cover. Without the seal, stores would not sell

Above: A graphic novel with art by John Buscema.

the comic books. Many people thought this was censorship, and violated the First Amendment, the right of free speech. The comic book industry felt they had to agree to this system to stay in business. Still, many comic book publishers and printers went bankrupt anyway. Artists, writers, inkers, and letterers were suddenly unemployed.

It was a sad time to be in comics, but John and Dolores did have some good news. In 1955, the

Above: John and Dolores Buscema on their wedding day, 1953.

couple welcomed their first child, daughter Dianne. While John was happy to be a new dad, he realized that he had to find work to support his family.

Turning away from crime and mystery, John went to Dell Comics and began working on *Roy Rogers and Trigger* comic books. However, he didn't enjoy creating this popular Western movie hero. John once said, "I did *Roy Rogers* for a few years, and hated it with a passion. I hated drawing Roy Rogers' face." But John went on to draw other cowboy-and-Indian comics, featuring such characters as The Cisco Kid and Indian Chief White Eagle.

John also produced some amazing comic books adapted from movies and television shows. Kids read wonderful graphic stories about such characters as the beautiful Helen of Troy, and Hercules, the strongest man in the world, as well as classic tales such as *The Count of Monte Cristo*. But by now John was tired of comic books. He began looking for something else.

Advertising

B y 1958, Buscema had been in the comic business for more than 10 years. His only break had been when he entered the United States Army during the Korean War in the early 1950s.

The time was right for a change. An opportunity opened up and John abandoned comics for advertising work at Chaite Studios, one of the largest advertising companies in New York City. He created illustrations and storyboards (rough sketches that show the scenes and shots for a television commercial) for the company's clients. John said, "It was a wonderful period of my life—I learned how to paint. I did a lot of things: I did paperback covers, layouts, editorial illustration, textbook illustrations, all kinds of stuff. I enjoyed it a lot."

Right: John Jr., John, Dolores, and Dianne Buscema on vacation in 1978.

Above: John at his drawing table, penciling a piece of art.

For six years, John worked in advertising, earning more money than he ever had in comics. It was a good time for the Buscema family, which was about to increase in size. In 1964, John, Dolores, and nine-year-old Dianne welcomed a baby boy, John, Jr., to the family.

The only problem was that John and his family lived several hours away from Buscema's busy job. John said, "My son was born in 1964, and for his first year I never saw him. I would get home and he'd be asleep. I would leave and he'd be asleep. The weekends would come around and I could go home, but I'd be working. It was a real cutthroat business."

Success in the 1960s

In 1966, John got a call from his old boss, Stan Lee, who was now the senior editor at Marvel Comics. Stan wanted Buscema back. Marvel had a number of successes in recent years:

Fantastic Four—1961
This superhero team featured four humans showered with cosmic rays, which gave them fantastic powers. Leader Reed Richards was "Mr. Fantastic," able to stretch like a rubber band. His future wife, Sue Storm, was "Invisible Woman." Johnny Storm could burst into flames and fly as "The Human Torch." Ben Grimm became the rock-like being known as "The Thing."

Spider-Man—1962
First appearing in *Amazing Fantasy #15,* this is the story of teenager Peter Parker, who was bitten by a radioactive spider and gained amazing spider-like abilities. The character received his own comic book, *The Amazing Spider-Man,* in 1963.

Above and *facing page:* Covers of best-selling Marvel comics, all penciled by John Buscema.

The Incredible Hulk — 1962
Scientist Bruce Banner, bombarded by gamma rays, turns from man to a hulking green monster when angered.

The Mighty Thor — 1962
Dr. Don Blake finds an ancient cane in a cave that transforms him into the Norse god of thunder.

The X-Men — 1963
Mutant humans with "X-tra" powers, led by telepath Professor Charles Xavier.

The Avengers — 1963
A group of top superheroes brought together to "fight the foes no single superhero could withstand."

John didn't realize it at the time, but he would work on all these successful comic books and many more in the years to come.

Back to Marvel

Since the comic industry had not been easy for Buscema, Stan Lee's phone call and job offer put John in a difficult position. Should he stay with advertising—which had paid him a nice salary and given him work he enjoyed—or return to the comic business?

Stan Lee pushed the great artist, offering him a chance to make slightly more money than John was making in advertising. The Marvel editor was quoted as saying, "John, things are different today. We're making a big comeback. Things are picking up…"

But what finally made Buscema make up his mind was something else: John could work at home. He wouldn't have to drive to work. He could actually see his family during the day. John decided to return to comics and Marvel.

Buscema began penciling his first comic book. However, after so many years out of the business, John discovered that even an experienced artist like himself could have problems. John stated, "You can do illustration, you can do layouts, but that doesn't mean you can do comics. It's a whole different ball game."

John felt he'd done a bad job on that first comic book, which Buscema remembers being *The Incredible Hulk*. Stan Lee had a solution, the same fix he'd performed with many other Marvel artists. He gave John a stack of comics produced by Jack "King" Kirby, one of the top artists in the industry.

John studied Kirby's layouts, including the pacing (the introduction of a new scene or character), the panels, the angles, and the "look" of Kirby's work. John knew what to do. He said, "I started working from them, and that's what saved me."

Above: After moving into the advertising field in 1958, "Big" John Buscema returned to comics in 1966.

Above: Jack Kirby, often called "The King of Comics," stands in front of artwork he created for Marvel's popular comic, *The Fantastic Four.*

When Buscema needed help on a panel, he looked over Jack's work. Jack knew how to make amazing action, and that's what comic book readers wanted. During the months when John was re-learning the comic business, he was smart enough to learn from the very best. From explosions to people flying, he used Jack's basic layouts, rearranged them, and created wonderful graphic stories. "Stan was happy. The editors were happy, so I was happy." And John would make millions of fans happy as well.

Marvel Success

Buscema had re-started his career by studying and working from Jack Kirby's "break-downs"—very simple pencil sketches. A few months later, in 1967, John was given his first full-book assignment: *The Avengers*. It was also his first superhero "group" book.

Picking up from the initial work of Jack Kirby and artist Don Heck, John found *The Avengers* to be quite a challenge. But, for several years, John created amazing tales surrounding an ever-changing group of superheroes who varied issue-to-issue and year-to-year. From founding members Thor, The Incredible Hulk, Ant-Man, The Wasp, Iron Man, and Captain America, the series evolved to include many different popular Marvel characters. John had to find a way to incorporate all the characters, without overwhelming the readers. It was difficult, but he did the job well.

Right: John Buscema at work in his studio. Comic books sit on a nearby table.

Above: The Avengers #43 was one of John Buscema's first team comics for Marvel. This August 1967 issue featured superheroes Scarlet Witch, Captain America, Goliath, Wasp, and Quicksilver.

Above: The Avengers #302. This April 1989 cover was also drawn by John Buscema. It featured superheroes Captain America, Invisible Woman, Mr. Fantastic, The Mighty Thor, and Gilgamesh.

As John felt more comfortable producing comics, he began working on many different books in the Marvel library, including *The Incredible Hulk* and *The X-Men.* At first he worked from a pre-written script, but as he became more comfortable with the characters, he began using what was dubbed as "The Marvel Method." John would talk to Stan Lee and say, "Stan, I'm ready for a plot. What have you got in mind?" From the basic story outline, John would create the pictures. The words would be placed later. Many of the great Marvel artists worked in this manner, but it definitely required an experienced artist who knew how to blend words and pictures. Since John was now such an artist, his work continued to grow.

The Silver Surfer

In 1968, John had the chance to bring back Silver Surfer, a character introduced a few years earlier by Jack Kirby and Stan Lee. The co-creators had begun the character's history:

"When the beautiful world of Zenn-La is attacked by planet-eating alien Galactus, young astronomer Norrin Radd volunteers to become the super being's herald, or helper. Radd will find empty worlds that can be eaten by Galactus to fill his great hunger.

"Galactus spares Radd's homeland and gives the young man cosmic powers, a special silvery appearance and a surfboard-like vehicle. As time passes, Radd discovers that it is difficult to find planets to feed Galactus.

"Silver Surfer thinks Earth may be okay to eat, but a blind sculptress, Alicia Masters, convinces Surfer otherwise. Surfer stands with the Fantastic Four against his master. Galactus spares Earth, but to punish his ungrateful herald, he puts an energy barrier around the planet that will keep Surfer from leaving."

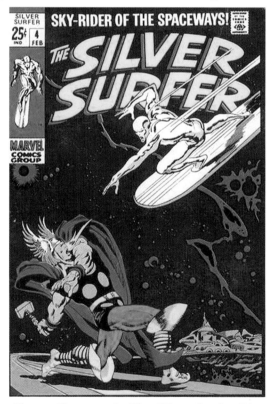

Above: Buscema's *The Silver Surfer #4.*

Above: Artist John Buscema with Marvel writer, creator, and editor, Stan Lee, 1988.

From this somewhat complex story, Buscema and Lee worked on several comic books. But, for whatever the reason, Silver Surfer never took off. Jack Kirby was unhappy about not being able to work on it. Stan Lee didn't know where to take the stories. Buscema remembered being very proud of *The Silver Surfer* #4, but he also recalled that editor Stan Lee disliked it.

For a period of time, Silver Surfer only made guest appearances in other comic books. He would later return successfully, but John Buscema had another hero to think about.

Conan the Barbarian

Different artists enjoy drawing different things. Some find superheroes fun. Some enjoy drawing "bad guys." John Buscema liked drawing animals, but he loved drawing mythological places and beings. That brought him to the *Conan the Barbarian* series in the 1970s.

The Conan character was originally created by Robert E. Howard in the 1930s. Set in a mythical earthly time, the great warrior experienced adventure after adventure. When John read some of the stories, he knew he wanted to work on them: "I fell in love with them as soon as I read them. I was chomping at the bit, I wanted to do them so badly."

Unfortunately, Buscema was paid a lot of money, and Marvel publisher Martin Goodman did not want John to work on something this new. Conan might fail, and if it did, the company would lose a lot of money. To John's disappointment, another artist, Barry Windsor-Smith, created the first issues.

Above: Conan The Barbarian #44, one of Buscema's first issues of this character.

Left: John Buscema draws Conan, one of his favorite characters, at a comics convention in 1999.

Once the character was established, however, John was brought in to work on the tales, along with writer Roy Thomas. John loved it. "I had a lot of freedom in those books. I could do anything with buildings and create costumes," John said.

John's enjoyment showed in his work. He received the 1974 Academy of Comic Book Arts Award as Best Penciller (Dramatic) for his work on *Conan the Barbarian*.

The Marvel Way

John wasn't the only Buscema working at Marvel. His younger brother, Silvio "Sal" Buscema, worked at Marvel as well. As an inker—someone who used black ink to make clear, clean black lines over rough pencil sketches—Sal did many of John's comic pages, as well as penciling some of his own comics. John was glad to have his brother on board, and once mentioned that Sal was one of his favorite inkers.

Right: John Buscema (striped shirt) stands next to brother, Al. Sal Buscema (pink shirt), who also worked at Marvel Comics, stands next to their sister, Carole.

Above: Internationally known artist John Buscema is surrounded by many young comic book fans in a shop in Italy.

Below: How To Draw Comics The Marvel Way, by Stan Lee and John Buscema, became one of the best instruction books on creating comics ever produced. It was later made into a DVD, starring Lee and Buscema.

For a while, it seemed that nearly every Marvel comic seemed to have one Buscema or the other in the credits.

Influencing not only his brother, John Buscema also taught comic book drawing to many young people. He began his own small school in a New York hotel. Stan Lee visited one of John's classes, and with Stan pushing, the artist and the editor created one of the top drawing books of all time: *How To Draw Comics The Marvel Way.* First published in 1978, it is still available nearly 30 years later. The two comic book pros also produced a DVD version.

Michelangelo of Comics

In 1996, Buscema "retired," but continued working on different projects. He also became a popular figure at comic book conventions. John kept teaching others, even when he became sick.

Right: John Buscema drawing at a comics convention.

In the fall of 2001, John Buscema was diagnosed with stomach cancer. On January 10, 2002, only a month after he turned 74, "Big" John Buscema died, leaving behind a larger-than-life legacy.

For more than 50 years, John penciled amazing art. During the course of his 30-plus years at Marvel, From #1 issues (such as *Ka-Zar*), to building on other artists' beginnings (such as *The Avengers*), John Buscema worked on nearly every major Marvel comic book. His imagination, talent, and his love of the art form earned John a nickname: the Michelangelo of Comics.

It's a fitting tribute to Buscema to be linked to one of his own idols — a master artist of the ages. John Buscema, himself, will also be remembered and forever treasured as a creator, a teacher, and an amazing master of the human form.

Left: The Michelangelo of Comics, John Buscema, and some of his popular comic book covers.

Glossary

Censorship
The control of what is written or spoken by a central authority, often a government or large group of outspoken individuals.

Comics Code Authority (CCA)
Established in 1954 as a way for comic book publishers to deal with parents' concerns about the effects of crime and horror comics on kids. Every comic book published required the CCA's seal of approval, and had to follow a strict set of guidelines. The code is still in use today, although not all comic books are published with the CCA seal.

Deadlines
When a job or project must be completed. Usually an amount of time or specific date.

Illustrate
To add a piece of art to a printed story. The art may be a drawing, painting, or photo.

Inker
An artist who uses a pen or brush to apply black ink to roughly drawn ("penciled") comic book pages in order to create clean, clear lines.

Juvenile Delinquency
A juvenile is a young person, usually under the age of 18. Delinquency means acting antisocially, or breaking the law. In the mid-1950s, many people thought comic books that showed a lot of violence or antisocial behavior caused children to become juvenile delinquents. This debate is being argued again today, with violent video games taking the place of comic books.

Korean War

A civil war between North and South Korea that was fought from 1950 to 1953. The United States supported South Korea.

Layouts

The way in which the words and/or pictures are laid out on a page.

Leonardo da Vinci

An Italian artist, engineer, and scientist who lived from 1452 to 1519. He studied and produced notebooks of materials on human biology, as well as ideas for an aircraft and a submarine. One of his most famous works is the painting of the *Mona Lisa*.

Michelangelo

Michelangelo Buonarroti was an Italian artist and sculptor who lived from 1475 to 1564. He is well known for his work on the human form. One of his most famous pieces is David, the statue of the Biblical hero.

Penciller

An artist who draws the rough pencil lines for comic book art.

Storyboards

A number of simple drawings that roughly outline a commercial, cartoon, or film. Each drawing usually includes production directions and whatever speaking parts will be heard.

Superheroes

Characters, often human, but they may also be alien or mythological beings, who develop or have special skills that give them superhuman powers. These characters use their powers for good, helping and protecting people.

Left: In this photo, taken in 2000, John Buscema sits with his granddaughter in his den, surrounded by some of his artwork and awards.

Index